Teach Me How to Pray

(Praying with Confidence)

By: Dr. Darrell D. Cummings PhD

Dedication

This book is dedicated to everyone who has supported me over my years in ministry.

I would also like to thank my church family who allows me to go to the nations:

Thank you (Maranatha Ministries International) for all your prayers and support.

Special thanks to:

Min Dre Adams (PPA) for his efforts in helping to complete this book.

To God be, the Glory!

Special Thanks

Maranatha Church, Spartanburg, SC

The Centre Church, San Bernardino, CA

Spirit of Faith Christian Center Oxon Hill, MD

Garden Grove Church of God, Garden Grove, CA

Word Alive Church DE

_____

And to my family, I love you and would not be able to do this without you.

Contents

Introduction

Prayer is a lost art in modern times, but it is an essential art for believers to have a powerful, potent, and dynamic prayer life. A powerful prayer life produces a closer relationship with God, a different and optimistic view of the world around us, and a confidence in oneself and God that is unshakeable. Through the years of being a Christian and serving in ministry, I learned that the most powerful impact in a believer's life is prayer, but even more so than just prayer is praying the word of God. Praying the word of God is praying the will of God. The will of God is made known to man through the scriptures. The scriptures declare infallible and unshakeable truths.

The Bible says we have not because we ask not, and at times when we ask, we ask a miss. By praying the word of God, we virtually excuse ourselves of praying a miss as in James 4:3. Because of this we can have confidence that our prayers are heard and are in concert with the will of God; therefore, we know our prayers are answered.

Things to Know
When You Pray

Believe that you receive what you ask for

Mark 11:22-24

Have faith in God, Jesus answered. Truly I tell you, if anyone says to this mountain, 'Go, throw yourself into the sea,' and does not doubt in their heart but believes that what they say will happen, it will be done for them. Therefore I tell you, whatever you ask for in prayer, believe that you have received it, and it will be yours.

This passage speaks of the confident attitude that's required when one approaches God in prayer.

This confident attitude is produced by the persistent dedication that the believer must have to pursue the person and presence of the Lord.

Romans 12:11

Never be lacking in zeal, but keep your spiritual fervor, serving the Lord.

It is impossible to have confidence in someone you do not know or in a thing that you have not experienced.

Jeremiah 29:13

You will seek me and find me when you seek me with all your heart

It is our responsibility as believers to come into a deep and enriching relationship with the father, we have access to the father through the life and blood of Jesus Christ. It is our responsibility and our privilege to search for his divine nature. It is also God's desire to have the same kind of relationship with us. "For God did not send his Son into the world to condemn the world, but to save the world through him." (John 3:17).

As we approach God in prayer we must take a position of great expectation based on our knowing and acknowledge his great ability to answer our prayer, not hoping that he will do as he already promised, but knowing that it's already done! "Before they call I will answer; while they are still speaking I will hear." (Isa 65:24). IS THERE ANYTHING TOO HARD FOR GOD?

Know all the promises of God are YES and AMEN

II Corinthians 1:20

For no matter how many promises God has made, they are "Yes" in Christ. And so through him the "Amen" is spoken by us to the glory of God.

In this text the 'yes' means I agree; and 'amen' means it's settled.

Isaiah 46:10

I make known the end from the beginning, from ancient times, what is still to come. I say, 'My purpose will stand, and I will do all that I please.'

I want to focus on Isaiah 46:10. Declaring the beginning from the end means that God went to the end of your life and prepared back to front so there will not be any mistakes. That's why in Jeremiah it says, "For I know the plans I have for you," declares the LORD, "plans to prosper you and not to harm you, plans to give you hope and a future." Seeing that God prepared your life from end to beginning should lead us to have confidence in (Jer. 29:11). I KNOW.

Know that you must find the promises of God in his word and pray (out loud) those promises back to him

---

John 15:7

If you remain in me and my words remain in you, ask whatever you wish, and it will be done for you.

God is not obligated to respond to anything other than his word

Isaiah 43:26

Review the past for me, let us argue the matter together; state the case for your innocence.

Psalms 103:20-22 (KJV)

Bless the LORD, ye his angels that excel in strength, that do his commandments, hearkening unto the voice of his word. Bless ye the LORD, all ye his hosts; ye ministers of his, that do his pleasure. Bless the LORD, all his works in all places of his dominion: bless the LORD, O my soul.

When praying, you have to identify the verses in the Bible that speak to the particular need that you have. Jesus said in the model prayer, "Your kingdom come your will be done on earth as it is in heaven." (Matt. 6:10).

We must make sure that our prayers are in concert with heaven.

Know that God rewards them who diligently seek Him

Hebrews 11:6

And without faith it is impossible to please God, because anyone who comes to him must believe that he exists and that he rewards those who earnestly seek him.

Hebrews 11 explains the innate nature of God, the Old Testament writers often referred to God as King, saying that His nature is kingly noble and royal.

1 Kings Chapter 10:1-29

When the queen of Sheba heard about the fame of Solomon and his relationship to the LORD, she came to test Solomon with hard questions. Arriving at Jerusalem with a very great caravan—with camels carrying spices, large quantities of gold, and precious stones—she came to Solomon and talked with him about all that she had on her mind. Solomon answered all her questions; nothing was too hard for the king to explain to her. When the queen of

Sheba saw all the wisdom of Solomon and the palace he had built, the food on his table, the seating of his officials, the attending servants in their robes, his cupbearers, and the burnt offerings he made at the temple of the LORD, she was overwhelmed.

She said to the king, "The report I heard in my own country about your achievements and your wisdom is true. But I did not believe these things until I came and saw with my own eyes. Indeed, not even half was told me; in wisdom and wealth you have far exceeded the report I heard. How happy your people must be! How happy your officials, who continually stand before you and hear your wisdom! Praise be to the LORD your God, who has delighted in you and placed you on the throne of Israel. Because of the LORD's eternal love for Israel, he has made you king to maintain justice and righteousness."

And she gave the king 120 talents of gold, large quantities of spices, and precious stones. Never again were so many spices brought in as those the queen of Sheba gave to King Solomon.

(Hiram's ships brought gold from Ophir; and from there they brought great cargoes of almugwood and precious stones. The king used the almugwood to make supports for the temple of the LORD and for the royal palace, and to make harps and lyres for the musicians. So much almugwood has never been imported or seen since that day.)

King Solomon gave the queen of Sheba all she desired and asked for, besides what he had given her out of his royal bounty. Then she left and returned with her retinue to her own country.

The weight of the gold that Solomon received yearly was 666 talents, not including the revenues from merchants and traders and from all the Arabian kings and the governors of the territories.

King Solomon made two hundred large shields of hammered gold; six hundred shekels of gold went into each shield. He also made three hundred small shields of hammered gold, with three minas of gold in each shield. The king put them in the Palace of the Forest of Lebanon.

Then the king made a great throne covered with ivory and overlaid with fine gold. The throne had six steps, and its back had a rounded top. On both sides of the seat were armrests, with a lion standing beside each of them. Twelve lions stood on the six steps, one at either end of each step. Nothing like it had ever been made for any other kingdom. All King Solomon's goblets were gold, and all the household articles in the Palace of the Forest of Lebanon were pure gold. Nothing was made of silver, because silver was considered of little value in Solomon's days. The king had a fleet of trading ships at sea along with the ships of Hiram. Once every three years it returned, carrying gold, silver and ivory, and apes and baboons.

King Solomon was greater in riches and wisdom than all the other kings of the earth. The whole world sought audience with Solomon to hear the wisdom God had put in his heart. Year after year, everyone who came brought a gift—articles of silver and gold, robes, weapons and spices, and horses and mules.

Solomon accumulated chariots and horses; he had fourteen hundred chariots and twelve thousand horses, which he kept in the chariot cities and also with him in Jerusalem. The king made silver as common in Jerusalem as stones, and cedar as plentiful as sycamore-fig trees in the foothills. Solomon's horses were imported from Egypt and from Kue—the royal merchants purchased them from Kue at the current price. They imported a chariot from Egypt for six hundred shekels of silver, and a horse for a hundred and fifty. They also exported them to all the kings of the Hittites and of the Arameans.

This chapter displays the nature of God's kingliness in the story of Solomon and the Queen of Sheba. God, like

Solomon did not allow the Queen of Sheba to out give him, "God is the king and no citizen of His kingdom will leave His presence with less than what they gave".

Know that God the one who hears your prayers is madly in love with you.

John 3:16

For God so loved the world that he gave his one and only Son, that whoever believes in him shall not perish but have eternal life.

God expressed His extreme and unrelenting passion toward us in the life and death of His Son. There is no higher expression that exists in our universe.

Matthew 23:37

Jerusalem, Jerusalem, you who kill the prophets and stone those sent to you, how often I have longed to gather your children together, as a hen gathers her chicks under her wings, and you were not willing.

John 15:13

Greater love has no one than this: to lay down one's life for one's friends.

1 John 4:9-11

This is how God showed his love among us: He sent his one and only Son into the world that we might live through him. This is love: not that we loved God, but that he loved us and sent his Son as an atoning sacrifice for our sins. Dear friends, since God so loved us, we also ought to love one another.

Know by being saved you have access to the Father in the name of Jesus and come boldly to the throne of grace.

John 16:23

In that day you will no longer ask me anything. Very truly I tell you, my Father will give you whatever you ask in my name.

Hebrews 4:16

Let us then approach God's throne of grace with confidence, so that we may receive mercy and find grace to help us in our time of need.

In Genesis 3, Adam disobeyed the commandment of God, giving way to the destruction and the perversion of our place of dominion disconnecting us from God by sin. God sent His Son Jesus in the form of men and became the sin payment for us; that is past, present, and future sin paid in full. That gives mankind access to the Father. When we stand before the Father in prayer He sees us through the payment of the blood of Jesus.

God is not mad at you. He loves you

John 16:23

In that day you will no longer ask me anything. Very truly I tell you, my Father will give you whatever you ask in my name.

Hebrews 4:16ESV

Therefore, while the promise of entering his rest still stands, let us fear lest any of you should seem to have failed to reach it.

Ephesians 2:12-14

Remember that at that time you were separate from Christ, excluded from citizenship in Israel and foreigners to the covenants of the promise, without hope and without God in the world. But now in Christ Jesus you who once were far away have been brought near by the blood of Christ. For he himself is our peace, who has made the two groups one and has destroyed the barrier, the dividing wall of hostility

Know that He will never turn away a broken and sincere heart.

Psalms 51:17

A broken heart is a heart of an individual who has run out of options; one who has tried his or her own way of living and utterly failed. That heart looks to God's wisdom to lead. God promises that He will never turn such a person away. When you pray you must be in agreement in your heart that God's plan is perfect. The only way to achieve that is to come to God with a broken and sincere heart.

Psalms 51:17

My sacrifice, O God, is a broken spirit; a broken and contrite heart you, God, will not despise.

Psalms 51:10

Create in me a pure heart, O God, and renew a steadfast spirit within me.

Know that the will of God is not automatic.

This particular truth is somewhat problematic to believers, some believe in the sovereignty of God. Sovereignty means that "God can do what He wants to when He wants to."

However, the Bible speaks to another truth. If God's will was automatic then everyone would be saved.

1 Timothy 2:3-4

This is good, and pleases God our Savior, who wants all people to be saved and to come to a knowledge of the truth.

Genesis 1:26

Then God said, "Let us make mankind in our image, in our likeness, so that they may rule over the fish in the sea and the birds in the sky, over the livestock and all the wild animals, and over all the creatures that move along the ground."

Psalms 115:16

The highest heavens belong to the LORD, but the earth he has given to mankind.

Psalms 8:6-9

You made them rulers over the works of your hands; you put everything under their feet: all flocks and herds, and the animals of the wild, the birds in the sky, and the fish in the sea, all that swim the paths of the seas. LORD, our Lord, how majestic is your name in all the earth!

In Genesis God gave mankind dominion authority and stewardship. God commanded them to be fruitful, multiply, replenish, and subdue. All of these things prove that the dominion of the earth truly belongs to men and what happens in the earth is a result of mankind's decisions.

So this means that God does not have legal right to impose His will in our lives.

The only way for God's will to be made manifest in the earth is for God to find a willing participant i.e. you and me, in the earth who will stand in agreement with His will that's in heaven to be made manifest in the earth. Jesus said it like this "Your kingdom come your will be done, in earth as it is in heaven". (Matt 6:10).

This is correct, however; the unfortunate truth is the world can fall into total disarray such as: pollution, global warming, wars, genocide, and so on and so forth. All of these horrific things happen in the dominion of men.

The statement above is referring to an individual's personal walk and development in his or her own life. It excludes the prophecies mentioned in the Scriptures; for example, what is found in the book of Revelation.

Deuteronomy 7:9

Know therefore that the LORD your God is God; he is the faithful God, keeping his covenant of love to a thousand generations of those who love him and keep his commandments.

Know that you must make time to pray.

Ecclesiastes 3:1

There is a time for everything, and a season for every activity under the heavens

Know that you must make time to pray, because life does not afford you the 'luxury' to do so.

Daniel believed so much in the power of prayer that he prayed three times a day. He created a pattern of prayer that produced power in his life.

Daniel 6:10

Now when Daniel learned that the decree had been published, he went home to his upstairs room where the windows opened toward Jerusalem. Three times a day he got down on his knees and prayed, giving thanks to his God, just as he had done before.

David said "Early will I rise to seek you."

Psalms 63:1

You, God, are my God, earnestly I seek you; I thirst for you, my whole being longs for you, in a dry and parched land where there is no water.

The person that you speak to first in the morning and last at night is the one that you are truly in love with.

Know that when you pray you must forgive

Mark 11:25

And when you stand praying, if you hold anything against anyone, forgive them, so that your Father in heaven may forgive you your sins.

Jesus explains very clearly in this scripture that forgiveness is key to prayers being answered.

Forgiveness at times is difficult but necessary,

Poachers in Africa have created a crude yet sophisticated trap to catch monkeys. They fashion a box and tie a string to ground it, they place a banana in the box and walk away. The prey sees the banana in the box and reaches for it clasping his hand around it. The monkey is trapped, the monkey is unwilling to let go of the banana if the monkey lets go of the banana he will be free, but his desire for the banana is more powerful than his desire to be free.

What are you holding on to?

Does it have you or do you have it?

Jesus said if you forgive others of their sins God will forgive you of yours,

Forgiveness is you not them.

LET IT GO!

Instructions

Some of you may be familiar with the prayer acronym A.C.T.S. It was formulated to give the believer a correct step-by-step procedure on how to approach the throne of grace in prayer. (Matt. 6:9-13). Each letter represents a specific topic during your prayer that you should address.

A-stands for Adoration
  (You begin to adore the Father in prayer)

C-stands for Confession
  (You confess your sins to the Father in prayer)

T-stands for Thanksgiving
  (You give thanks to the Father in prayer)

S-stands for Supplication
  (Make your petitions to the Father in prayer)

In this book you will be using the prayer acronym
C.A.C.T.S.C.

Both the C at the beginning and the end of the acronym
stands for confidence. I believe that praying with
confidence that is backed by the word of God is the most
effective way to approach the throne of grace.

C-stands for Confidence
  (Approach the throne with confidence)

A-stands for Adoration
  (You begin to adore the Father in prayer)

C-stands for Confession
  (You confess your sins to the Father in prayer)

T-stands for Thanksgiving
  (You give thanks to the Father in prayer)

S-stands for Supplication
  (Make your petitions to the Father in prayer)

C-stands for Confidence
  (Be confident your prayer is answered)

C.A.C.T.S.C. 1

Confidence

1 John 5: 14–15

And this is the confidence that we have in him, that if we ask anything according to his will, he hears us. And if we know that he hears us, whatsoever we ask, we know that we have the petitions that we desired of him. (KJV)

This is the confidence that I have in You (GOD) that if I ask anything according to your will, you listen to and hear me, and whatever I ask, I also know that I have the requests I made of you.

Adoration

Psalm 24:1, 2

The earth is the Lord's, and everything in it, the world, and all who live in it, for he founded it upon the seas and established it upon the waters. (NIV)

The earth and everything in it belongs to you. The world, and all who live in it, belong to you, for you founded it upon the seas and established it upon the waters.

Confession

Psalms 41:10–12

But You, O Lord, be merciful and gracious to me, and raise me up, that I may repay them. By this I know that you favor and delight in

me, because my enemy does not triumph over me. You have upheld my integrity and set me in your presence forever. (AMP)

Father be merciful and gracious to me, and raise me up, that I may repay them. By this I know that you favor and delight in me, because my enemy does not triumph over me. You uphold my integrity and set me in your presence forever.

Thanksgiving

Hebrews 12:28

Therefore, since we receive a kingdom that cannot be shaken, let us show gratitude, by which we may offer to God an acceptable service with reverence and awe. (NAS)

Now since I receive a kingdom that cannot be shaken, I show my gratitude, and I offer to you an acceptable service with reverence and awe.

Supplication

1 Kings 8:30

May you hear the humble and earnest requests from me and your people Israel when we pray toward this place. Yes, hear us from heaven where you live, and when you hear, forgive. (NLT)

Father you hear the humble and earnest requests from me when I pray toward this place. Yes, hear me from heaven where you live, and when you hear, you forgive.

Confidence

Jude 1:24

Now unto him who is able to keep you from falling, and to present you faultless before the presence of his glory with exceeding joy. (KJV)

Father I know you are able to keep me from falling, and to present me faultless before the presence of your glory with exceeding joy.

Prayer 1

Father this is the confidence that I have in you, that if I ask anything according to your will, you listen and hear me. And since I know that you listen to me in whatever I ask, I also know that I have the requests I made of you. Father I thank you that the earth and everything in it belongs to you. The world, and all who live in it, belong to you, for you founded it upon the seas and established it upon the waters. Now Father I ask you to be merciful and gracious to me, and raise me up, that I may repay them (my enemies). Through this I know that you favor and delight in me, because my enemy does not triumph over me. I thank you Father that you uphold my integrity and set me in your presence forever. Now because of your son Jesus, I receive a kingdom that cannot be shaken, I show my gratitude, and I offer to you an acceptable service with reverence and awe. I thank you Father because you hear the humble and earnest requests from me when I pray toward this place. You hear me from heaven where you live, and when you hear, you forgive. For I know you are able to keep me from falling, and to present me faultless before the presence of your glory with exceeding joy. In the name of Jesus Amen!

C.A.C.T.S.C. 2

Confidence

Hebrews 4:16

Let us therefore come boldly unto the throne of grace that we may obtain mercy, and find grace to help in time of need. (KJV)

Father I come boldly to your throne of grace that I may obtain mercy and find grace to help in time of need.

Adoration

Psalm 19:1

The heavens declare the glory of God, and the firmament shows his handiwork. (KJV)

The heavens declare your glory, and the firmament (sky) shows your handiwork.

Confession

1 John 1:9

If we confess our sins, he is faithful and just and will forgive us our sins and purify us from all unrighteousness. (NIV)

Lord you said if I confess my sins, you are faithful and just to forgive me of my sins and to cleanse me from all unrighteousness.

Thanksgiving

1 Chronicles 16:8

Give thanks to the LORD and proclaim his greatness. Let the whole world know what he has done. (NLT)

I give you thanks and proclaim your greatness. I let the whole world know what you have done.

Supplication

Psalm 119:170

May my supplication come before you; deliver me according to your promise. (NIV)

Father let my supplication come before you, and deliver me according to your promise.

Confidence

Philippians 1:6

For I am confident of this very thing, that He who began a good work in you will perfect it until the day of Christ Jesus. (NAS)

I am confident of this very thing, that You who began a good work in me will perfect it until the day of Christ Jesus.

Prayer 2

Heavenly Father I come boldly to your throne of grace, that I may obtain mercy and find the grace to help me in time of need. For it is written that the heavens declare your glory, and the sky shows your handiwork. Father you said if I confess my sins, you are faithful and just to forgive me of my sins and to cleanse me from all unrighteousness. I give you thanks and proclaim your greatness. I let the whole world know what you have done. Now in the name Jesus let my supplication come before you, and deliver me according to your promise. For I am confident of this very thing, that you who began a good work in me will perfect it until the day of Christ Jesus. In the name of Jesus Amen!

C.A.C.T.S.C. 3

Confidence

Hebrews 11:6

But without faith it is impossible to please him, for he that comes to God must believe that he is, and that he is a rewarder of them that diligently seek him. (KJV)

Father I know without faith it is impossible for me to please you, for your word says If I come to you, I must believe that you are, and because I diligently seek you, I will be rewarded.

Adoration

Psalm 40:5

O LORD my God, you have performed many wonders for us. Your plans for us are too numerous to list. You have no equal. If I tried to recite all your wonderful deeds, I would never come to the end of them. (NLT)

Father you have performed many wonders for me. Your plans for me are too numerous to list. You have no equal. If I tried to recite all your wonderful deeds, they would never end.

Confession

Titus 3:5

He saved us, not because of any works of righteousness that we had done, but because of His own pity and mercy, by [the] cleansing [bath] of the new birth (regeneration) and renewing of the Holy Spirit. (AMP)

You saved me, not because of any works of righteousness that I have done, but because of your own pity and mercy, by the cleansing of the new birth and renewing of the Holy Spirit.

Thanksgiving

Jonah 2:9

But I, with a song of thanksgiving, will sacrifice to you. What I have vowed I will make good. Salvation comes from the LORD. (NIV)

Now with a song of thanksgiving, will I sacrifice to you. What you have vowed you will make good. For salvation comes from you.

Supplication

1 Kings 8:52

May your eyes be open to my requests and to the requests of your people Israel. May you hear and answer them whenever they cry out to you. (NLT)

Father I pray that your eyes are open to my requests and to the requests of your people. I know that you hear me and answer whenever I cry out to you.

Confidence

Job 22:28

You shall also decree a thing, and it shall be established for you, and the light shall shine upon your ways. (KJV)

Father I know when I decree a thing, it shall be established for me, and your light shines upon my ways.

Prayer 3

Father I know without faith it is impossible for me to please you, for your word says if I come to you, I must believe that you are, and you reward me, because I diligently seek you. Father you have performed many wonders for me, and your plans for me are too numerous to list. You have no equal, and if I tried to recite all your wonderful deeds, they would never end. I thank you Father because you saved me, not because of any works of righteousness that I have done, but because of your own pity and mercy by the cleansing of the new birth and renewing of the Holy Spirit. And now with a song of thanksgiving, will I sacrifice to you, for what you have vowed you will make good. For I know salvation comes from you. I thank you Father that your eyes are open to my requests and to the requests of your people. I know that you hear me and answer whenever I cry out to you, and I know when I decree a thing, it shall be established for me, and your light shines upon my ways. In the name of Jesus Amen!

Confidence

Joshua 1:5

No man shall be able to stand before you all the days of your life; as I was with Moses, so I will be with you. I will not leave you nor forsake you. (NKJV)

Father your word says no man shall be able to stand before me all the days of my life; as you were with Moses, so shall you be with me. You will not leave me nor forsake me.

Adoration

Psalm 84:11

For the LORD God is a sun and shield; the LORD will give grace and glory; no good thing will he withhold from them that walk uprightly. (KJV)

For you God are a sun and shield, you give grace and glory, and no good thing will you withhold from me because I walk uprightly.

Confession

Galatians 2:20

I have been crucified with Christ and it is no longer I who live, but Christ lives in me. The life I now live in the body, I live by faith in the Son of God, who loved me and gave himself for me. (NIV)

I have been crucified with you and I no longer live, but you live in me. The life I now live in the body, I live by faith in you, who loved me and gave yourself for me.

Thanksgiving

Colossians 2:6–7

So then, just as you received Christ Jesus as Lord, continue to live in him, rooted and built up in him, strengthened in the faith as you were taught, and overflowing with thankfulness. (NIV)

Just as I received you as Lord, I continue to live in you, rooted and built up in you, strengthened in the faith as   I was taught, and I am overflowing with t h a n k f u l n e s s .

16

Supplication

Psalm 27:7

Hear my voice when I call, O LORD; be merciful to me and answer me. (NIV)

Hear my voice when I call, O LORD; be merciful to me and answer me. [Repeat of above; do you want to vary it slightly?]

Confidence

2 Corinthians 5:21

God made him who had no sin to be sin for us, so that in him we might become the righteousness of God. (NIV)

Father you made Jesus who knew no sin to become sin for me, that through Jesus I am the righteousness of you my God.

Prayer 4

Father your word says no man shall be able to stand before me all the days of my life; as you were with Moses, so shall you be with me. You will not leave me nor forsake me. For you are a sun and shield. You give grace and glory, and no good thing will you withhold from me because I walk uprightly. Father I am thankful that I have been crucified with you and I no longer live, but you live in me, and the life I now live in the body, I live by faith in you, who loved me and gave yourself for me. Now just as I received you as Lord, I continue to live in you, rooted and built up in you, strengthened in the faith as I was taught, and I am overflowing with thankfulness. Father I am thankful you hear my voice when I call, and you are merciful to me and you answer me. For you made Jesus who knew no sin to become sin for me, that through Jesus I am your righteousness. In the name of Jesus Amen!

C.A.C.T.S.C. 5

Confidence

Joshua 1:7

Only be strong and very courageous, that you may observe to do according to all the law that Moses my servant commanded you; do not turn from it to the right hand or to the left, that you may prosper wherever you go. (NKJV)

Father I am strong and very courageous, and I observe to do all that you commanded through your servant Moses (Word); I do not turn from it to the right or to the left, that I prosper everywhere I go.

Adoration

Psalm 95:4

In his hand are the deep places of the earth; the strength of the hills is his also. (KJV)

In your hand are the deep places of the earth; the strength of the hills is also yours.

Confession

1 Peter 3:9

Not returning evil for evil, or reviling for reviling, but on the contrary blessing, knowing that you were called to this, that you may inherit a blessing. (NKJV)

I do not repay evil with evil or insult with insult. But on the contrary, I repay evil with blessings, because this is my calling, that I may inherit the blessing.

Thanksgiving

Psalm 107:31

Let them give thanks to the LORD for his unfailing love and his wonderful deeds for mankind. (NIV)

I give continuous thanks to you my Lord for your unfailing love and your wonderful deeds for me.

Supplication

John 15:16

You did not choose me, but I chose you and appointed you to go and bear fruit—fruit that will last. Then   the

Father will give you whatever you ask in my name. (NIV)

I did not choose you, but you chose me and appointed me to go and bear fruit—fruit that will last. Then you will give me whatever I ask in your name.

Confidence

Joshua 1:9

Have I not commanded you? Be strong and of good courage; do not be afraid, nor be dismayed, for the Lord your God is with you wherever you go. (NKJV)

Father you have commanded me to be strong and of good courage, not be afraid, nor be dismayed, for you the Lord my God are with me wherever I go.

Prayer 5

Father in you I am strong and very courageous, and I observe to do all that you commanded through your word; I do not turn from it to the right or to the left, so that I prosper everywhere I go. Father in your hand are the deep places of the earth; the strength of the hills is also yours. I thank you for the strength to not repay evil with evil or insult with insult, but on the contrary, I repay evil with blessings, for this is my calling, that I may inherit the blessing. I give you continuous thanks for your unfailing love and your wonderful deeds for me. For I know I did not choose you, but you chose me and appointed me to go and bear fruit—fruit that will last. Then you will give me whatever I ask in your name. For your word has commanded me to be strong and of good courage, not be afraid, nor be dismayed, for you the Lord my God are with me wherever I go. In the name of Jesus Amen!

C.A.C.T.S.C. 6

Confidence

Numbers 23:19

God is not a man, that he should lie; neither the son of man, that he should repent. Has he said, and shall he not do it? Or has he spoken, and shall he not make it good? (KJV)

Father you are not a man, that you would lie, nor are you the son of man, that you would have to repent. If you said it, you will do it. If you spoke it, you will make it good. Behold you have given a command for me to bless me, and that blessing cannot be overturned or denied.

Adoration

Psalm 33:6–9

By the word of the Lord were the heavens made, and all their host by the breath of His mouth.

He gathers the waters of the sea as in a bottle; He puts the deeps in storage places. Let all the earth fear the Lord; let all the inhabitants of the world stand in awe of Him. For He spoke and it was done; He commanded, and it stood fast. (AMP)

By your word the heavens were made, and all of the host of heaven by the breath of your mouth. You gather the waters of the sea as in a bottle; you put the deeps in storage places. All the earth fears you; all the inhabitants of the world stand in awe of you. For you spoke and it was done; you commanded, and it stood fast.

Confession

Psalms 51: 1–2

Have mercy upon me, O God, according to your loving-kindness; according to the multitude of your tender mercies, blot out my transgressions. Wash me thoroughly from my iniquity, and cleanse me from my sin. (NKJV)

Father have mercy upon me, according to your loving-kindness, and according your tender mercies, blot out my transgressions. Wash me thoroughly from my iniquity, and cleanse me from my sin.

Thanksgiving

Psalms 34:1

I will bless the LORD at all times: his praise shall continually be in my mouth. (KJV)

I bless your name at all times; your praise is continually in my mouth.

Supplication

Psalm 28:2

Hear my cry for mercy as I call to you for help, as I lift up my hands toward your most holy place. (NIV)

Father you hear my cry for mercy as I call to you for help, as I lift up my hands toward your most holy place.

Confidence

Psalms 20:7

Some trust in chariots, and some in horses, but we trust in the name of the LORD our God. (NIV)

Some trust in chariots, and some in horses, but I will trust in the name of the Lord my God.

Prayer 6

Father you are not a man, that you would lie, nor are you the son of man, that you would have to repent. If you said it, you will do it. If you spoke it, you will make it good. For behold you have given a command to bless me, and that blessing cannot be overturned or denied. For by your word the heavens were made, and all of host of heaven by the breath of your mouth. You gather the waters of the sea as in a bottle; you put the deeps in storage places. All the earth fears you; all the inhabitants of the world stand in awe of you. For you spoke and it was done; you commanded, and it stood fast. Now Father have mercy upon me, according to your loving-kindness, and according your tender mercies, blot out my transgressions. Wash me thoroughly from my iniquity, and cleanse me from my sin. For this cause I bless your name at all times, and your praise is continually in my mouth. I thank you Father. I know you hear my cry for mercy as I call to you for help, as I lift up my hands toward your most holy place. There are some who trust in chariots, and some in horses, but I will trust in the name of the Lord my God. In the name of Jesus Amen!

Confidence

Joshua 1:8

Keep this Book of the Law always on your lips; meditate on it day and night, so that you may be careful to do everything written in it. Then you will be prosperous and successful. (NIV)

I keep this Book of the Law on my lips at all times; I meditate on it day and night, and I am careful to do everything written in it. For through this I make my way prosperous, and have good success.

Adoration

Psalm 8:1

O Lord, our Lord, how excellent is your name in all the earth, who have set your glory above the heavens. (NKJV)

O Lord, my God, how excellent is your name in all the earth! For you have set your glory above the heavens.

Confession

Psalm 139:1–4

You have searched me, LORD, and you know me. You know when I sit and when I rise; you perceive my thoughts from afar. You discern my going out and my lying down; you are familiar with all my ways. Before a word is on my tongue, you, LORD, know it completely. (NIV)

You search me, LORD, and you know me. You know when I sit and when I rise; you perceive my thoughts from afar.

You discern my going out and my lying down; you are familiar with all my ways. Before a word is on my tongue, you, LORD, know it completely.

Thanksgiving

Psalms 69:30

I will praise the name of God with a song, and will magnify him with thanksgiving. (NKJV)

I praise your name with a song, and I magnify you with thanksgiving.

Supplication

Mark 11:22–25

"Have faith in God," Jesus answered. "I tell you the truth, if anyone says to this mountain, 'Go, throw yourself into the sea,' and does not doubt in his heart but believes that what he says will happen, it will be done for him. Therefore, I tell you, whatever you ask for in prayer, believe that you have received it, and it will be yours. (NIV)

I have faith in you, and if I say to this mountain, 'Go, throw yourself into the sea,' and I do not doubt in my heart but believe that what I say will happen, it will be done for me. And whatever I ask for in prayer, I believe that I have received it and it is mine.

Confidence

Proverbs 18:20

From the fruit of his mouth a man's stomach is filled; with the harvest from his lips he is satisfied. (NIV)

Father I know by the fruit of my mouth my stomach is filled, and with the harvest from my lips I am satisfied.

Prayer 7

Father I keep this Book of the Law on my lips at all times; I meditate on it day and night, and I am careful to do everything written in it. For through this I make my way prosperous, and have good success. I bless your name for it is excellent in all the earth, and you have set your glory above the heavens. Search me, O Lord, and know me. You know when I sit and when I rise; you perceive my thoughts from afar. You discern my going out and my lying down; you are familiar with all my ways. Before a word is on my tongue, you know it completely. So I praise your name with a song, and I magnify you with thanksgiving. For   I have faith in you, and if I say to this mountain, "Go, throw yourself into the sea," and I do not doubt in my heart, but believe what I say will happen, it is done for me. And whatever I ask for in prayer, I believe that I have received it and it is mine. And I am thankful that I know by the fruit of my mouth my stomach is filled, and with the harvest from my lips I am satisfied. In the name of Jesus Amen!

C.A.C.T.S.C. 8

Confidence

Romans 8:39

Neither height nor depth, nor anything else in all creation, will be able to separate us from the love of God that is in Christ Jesus our Lord. (NIV)

Father I know that no height, no depth, nor any other created thing, shall be able to separate me from your love which is in Christ Jesus my Lord.

Adoration

Psalm 86:8, 10

Among the gods there is none like unto thee, O Lord; neither are there any works like unto thy works. For thou art great, and do wondrous things: thou art God alone. (KJV)

Father there is no other god like you; neither are there any works like yours. For you are great, and do wondrous things, for you are God alone.

Confession

Romans 3:23

For all have sinned, and come short of the glory of God. (KJV)

For I like all have sinned and come short of your glory.

Thanksgiving

1 Thessalonians 5:18

Thank [God] in everything [no matter what the circumstances may be, be thankful and give thanks], for this is the will of God for you [who are] in Christ Jesus [the Revealer and Mediator of that will]. (AMP)

Father I thank you in everything, for this is your will in Christ Jesus for me.

Supplication

Philippians 4:6

Don't worry about anything; instead, pray about everything. Tell God what you need, and thank him for all he has done. (NLT)

I don't worry about anything, but instead, I pray about everything, and tell you what I need, and thank you for all you've done.

Confidence

Romans 8:37

No, in all these things we are more than conquerors through him who loved us. (NIV)

Father I know in all these things I am more than a conqueror through you who loved me and give yourself for me.

Prayer 8

Father I know that no height, no depth, nor any other created thing, can separate me from your love which is in Christ Jesus. For there is no other god like you; neither are there any works like yours. You are great, and you do wondrous things, for you are God alone. I thank you for your mercy, for I like everyone have sinned and come short of your glory. And regardless of my circumstance I thank you in everything, for this is your will in Christ Jesus for me. I don't worry about anything, but instead, I pray about everything, and tell you what I need and thank you for all you've done. For I know in all these things I am more than a conqueror through you who loved me and gave yourself for me. In the name of Jesus Amen!

C.A.C.T.S.C. 9

Confidence

John 10:27

My sheep hear my voice, and I know them, and they follow me. (KJV)

I am your sheep and I hear your voice, and you know me, and I follow you.

Adoration

Psalm 93:1, 2

The LORD reigns; he is robed in majesty; the LORD is robed in majesty and is armed with strength. The world is firmly established; it cannot be moved. Your throne was established long ago; you are from all eternity. (NIV)

Father you reign; you are robed in majesty and armed with strength. Because of you the world is firmly established, and it cannot be moved. Your throne was established long ago, for you are from all eternity.

Confession

Psalms 51 9:10

Hide thy face from my sins, and blot out all mine iniquities. Create in me a clean heart and renew a right spirit within me. (KJV)

Father hide your face from my sins, and blot out all mine iniquities. Create in me a clean heart and renew a right spirit within me.

Thanksgiving

Psalms 95:2

Let us come before him with thanksgiving and extol him with music and song. (NIV)

I come before you with thanksgiving and extol you with music and song.

Supplication

Romans 8:26

In the same way, the Spirit helps us in our weakness. We do not know what we ought to pray for, but the Spirit himself intercedes for us with groans that words cannot express. (NIV)

In the same way, the Spirit helps me in my weakness. I do not know what I ought to pray for, but the Spirit himself intercedes for me with groans that words cannot express.

Confidence

John: 14:17

The Spirit of truth, whom the world cannot receive, because it neither sees Him nor knows Him, but you know Him, for He dwells with you and will be in you. (NKJV)

I have the Spirit of truth, someone the world cannot receive, because it neither sees you or knows you, but I know you, because you live in me.

Prayer 9

Father I know that I am your sheep and I hear your voice; you know me, and I follow you. I adore you because you reign. You are robed in majesty and armed with strength. Because of you the world is firmly established, and it cannot be moved. Your throne was established long ago, for you are from all eternity. Father I pray that you hide your face from my sins, and blot out all my iniquities. Create in me a clean heart and renew a right spirit within me. I give you praise and I come before you with thanksgiving and extol you with music and song. Father the Holy Spirit helps me in my weakness. Seeing that I do not know what I ought to pray for, but the Holy Spirit himself intercedes for me with groans that words cannot express. I thank you that I have the Spirit of truth, someone the world cannot receive, because it neither sees you nor knows you, but I know you, because you live in me. In the name of Jesus Amen!

C.A.C.T.S.C. 10

Confidence

Ephesians 6:10–17

Finally, my brethren, be strong in the Lord and in the power of His might. Put on the whole armor of God, that you may be able to stand against the wiles of the devil. For we do not wrestle against flesh and blood, but against principalities, against powers, against the rulers of the darkness of this age, against spiritual hosts of wickedness in the heavenly places.

Therefore. take up the whole armor of God that you may be able to withstand in the evil day, and having done all, to stand. Stand therefore, having girded your waist with truth, having put on the breastplate of righteousness, and having shod your feet with the preparation of the gospel of peace; above all, taking the shield of faith with which you will be able to quench all the fiery darts of the wicked one. And take the helmet of salvation, and the sword of the Spirit, which is the word of God. (NKJV)

Father I am strong in you and in the power of your might. I put on the whole armor of God that I may be able to stand against the wiles of the devil. For I now know I do not wrestle against flesh and blood, but against principalities, against powers, against the rulers of the darkness of this age, against spiritual hosts of wickedness in the heavenly places. I put on the whole armor of God, that I may be able to withstand in this evil day, and having done all, to stand. I stand therefore, having girded my waist with truth, having put on the breastplate of righteousness, and having shod my feet with the preparation of the gospel of peace; above all, I take the shield of faith with which I will be able to quench all the fiery darts of the wicked one. And I put on the helmet of salvation, and I take the sword of the Spirit, which is the word of God.

Adoration

Psalm 100:1–3

Make a joyful noise unto the LORD, all ye lands. Serve the LORD with gladness: come before his presence with singing. Know ye that the LORD he is God: it is he that hath made us, and not we ourselves; we are his people, and the sheep of his pasture. (KJV)

I make a joyful noise unto you. I serve you with gladness. I come before your presence with singing. I know you the LORD are God; it is you that made me, and not I myself; I am your people, and the sheep of your pasture.

Confession

Psalms 51: 7

Purge me with hyssop, and I shall be clean; wash me, and I shall be whiter than snow. (KJV)

I am guilty of sin, but you purge me with hyssop (herb), and I am clean; you wash me, and I am whiter than snow.

Thanksgiving

Ephesians 5:20

Giving thanks always for all things unto God and the Father in the name of our lord Jesus Christ. (KJV)

I give thanks always for all things unto you and in the name of Jesus Christ.

Supplication

Psalms 51:11–12

Cast me not away from thy presence, and take not thy Holy Spirit from me. Restore unto me the joy of thy salvation, and uphold me with thy free spirit.

Father cast me not away from your presence, and take not your Holy Spirit from me, but restore unto me the joy of your salvation, and uphold me with your free spirit.

Confidence

Romans 8:30

And those he predestined, he also called; those he called, he also justified; those he justified, he also glorified. (NIV)

Father your words says those who you predestined, you also called; those who you called, you also justified; and those who you justified, you also glorified.

Prayer 10

Father in adoration I make a joyful noise unto you. I serve you with gladness; I come before your presence with singing. For I know you are God. Father I thank you that I am strong in you and in the power of your might. I now put on the whole armor of God that I may be able to stand against the wiles of the devil. For I know I do not wrestle against flesh and blood, but against principalities, against powers, against the rulers of the darkness of this age, against spiritual hosts of wickedness in heavenly places. I put on the whole armor of God that I may be able to withstand in these evil days, and having done all, to stand. I stand therefore, having girded my waist with truth, having put on the breastplate of righteousness, and having shod my feet with the preparation of the gospel of peace; above all, I take the shield of faith and with it I am able to quench all the fiery darts of the wicked one. And I put on the helmet of salvation, and I take the sword of the spirit, which is the word of God. Father purge me with hyssop (herb), and I shall be clean; wash me, and I shall be whiter than snow, and I give thanks for all things unto you in the name of Jesus Christ. Father cast me not away from your presence, and take not your Holy Spirit from me, but restore unto me the joy of your salvation, and uphold me with your free spirit. For your word says those who you predestined, you also called; those who you called, you also justified; and those who you justified, you also glorified. In the name of Jesus Amen!

Build Your Own Pray

Choose a Bible text from the concordance in the back of this book. Modify the text and make it about you (in the first person). See the examples earlier this book.

Exchange words like 'our', 'us', and 'them' to 'my' and 'me'.

Example:
Supplication

Original
1 Kings 8:30

May you hear the humble and earnest requests from me and your people Israel when we pray toward this place. Yes, hear us from heaven where you live, and when you hear, forgive. (NLT)

Modified
1 Kings 8:30

Father you hear the humble and earnest requests from me when I pray toward this place. Yes, hear me from heaven where you live, and when you hear, you forgive.

Afterward, put the whole prayer together and read it out loud; and remember to read it with confidence.

C.A.C.T.S.

C-stands for Confidence (Approach the throne with confidence)

_____

_____

_____

_____

_____

A-stands for Adoration (You begin to adore the Father in prayer)

_____

_____

_____

_____

_____

C-stands for Confession (You confess your sins to the Father in prayer)

_____

_____

_____

_____

_____

T-stands for Thanksgiving (You give thanks to the Father in prayer)

_____

_____

_____

_____

_____

_____

S-stands for Supplication (Make your petitions to the Father in prayer)

_____

_____

_____

_____

_____

_____

C-stands for Confidence (Be confident your prayer is answered)

_____

_____

_____

_____

_____

To help you build your own prayer, utilize the concordance

CONFIDENCE	ADORATION	CONFESSION
2 Chronicles 32:8	Exodus 3:5	2 Chronicles 7:14
Nehemiah 6:16	Deuteronomy 6:5	Psalms 32:51
Psalm 71:5	Deuteronomy 10:12	Psalms 34:14
Proverbs 3:26	Deuteronomy 11:1	Psalms 38:18
Proverbs 31:11	Deuteronomy 13:4	Psalms 41:4
Isaiah 32:17	Joshua 5:15	Psalm 51:1-3
Jeremiah 17:7	Joshua 22:5	Psalms 69:5
2 Corinthians 2:3	1 Chronicles 16:29	Isaiah 55:6-7
2 Corinthians 3:4	Psalm 5:7	Jeremiah 25:5
Ephesians 3:12	Psalm 18:1	Jeremiah 26:3
Philippians 3:3	Psalm 26:8	Ezekiel 18:21-23
2 Thessalonians 3:4	Psalm 29:2	Jonah 3:10
Hebrews 3:14	Psalm 31:23	Mark 1:15
Hebrews 4:16	Psalm 33:8	Luke 13:3
Hebrews 10:19	Psalm 95:6	Acts 3:19
Hebrews 10:35	Psalm 99:5	Acts 8:22
Hebrews 13:6	Psalm 116:1	Romans 10:9-10
1 John 3:21	Isaiah 6:3	2 Peter 3:9
1 John 4:17	Daniel 6:26	Revelation 2:5
1 John 5:14	Habakkuk 2:20	Revelation 3:19

on the next two pages.

THANKSGIVING	SUPPLICATION
1 Chronicles 16:8	1 Kings 8:28
1 Chronicles 29:13	1 Kings 8:38
Psalm 9:1	1 Kings 8:45
Psalm 20:4	1 Kings 8:49
Psalm 30:12	1 Kings 8:54
Psalm 95:2	1 Kings 9:3
Psalm 100:4	2 Chronicles 6:19
Psalm 105:1	2 Chronicles 6:29
Psalm 106:1	2 Chronicles 6:35
Psalm 107:1	Psalms 55:1
Isaiah 12:4-5	Daniel 9:17
Romans 1:21	Matthew 6: 9-13
2 Corinthians 9:15	Acts 1:14
Ephesians 5:20	Romans 8:26
Philippians 4:6	Ephesians 6:18
Colossians 3:15	Philippians 4:6
Colossians 3:17	Hebrews 4:16
Colossians 4:2	James 5:13
1 Thessalonians 5:18	James 5:16
Philemon 1:4	1 Peter 5:7

About the Author

A native of Washington, D.C., and residing in Inland Empire, CA, Dr. Darrell D. Cummings received Jesus as Lord and Savior at the age of six. At the age of thirteen, he was called to the ministry. He has a Bachelor's of Theology, a Master's of Divinity, Doctorate of Humanities, and a Doctorate of Religious Philosophy. Dr. Cummings is the founder and Overseer of Maranatha Ministries International in Spartanburg, South Carolina. Part of his ministry is conducting conferences and workshops around the United States, to equip and empower the saints to move into their prophetic callings and giftings. Dr. Cummings has been blessed to minister nationally and is known as a true Prophet of God. He flows in the gifts of the Spirit such as the word of wisdom, word of knowledge, prophecy and gifts of healing, etc. He also serves as a mentor to many pastor and ministers around the globe. He believes every word that proceeds out of the mouth of God, and the Holy Scriptures. Dr. Cummings is a great musician and vocalist participating in several national Gospel recordings and has just released his first solo album entitled "Open Heaven". He is also a very proud father of four children. His desire is to see every believer walk in the fullness of their God-given potential, and lack in nothing!

IF THIS BOOK HAS BEEN A BLESSING IN YOUR LIFE
PLEASE LET US KNOW

 www.thedcministrie.org

 Instagram/dcministries

 facebook.com/Dr-Darrell-D-Cummings

 @dcministries

 twitter.com/dcmin_inc

Made in the USA
Charleston, SC
17 November 2015